Speak To Your Glue

By Anika S. Madison

Speak To Your Glue

©2022

All rights reserved. First Edition

This book is for anyone who feels stuck and unable to move forward. You are working towards realizing your passions, but there is a powerful glue keeping you from this realization.

For the purposes of this book, the definition for the glue is anything that you are stuck to that prevents beneficial action.

I am not referring to the glue that you can wash off with soap and water. If you stepped into the kind of glue I am referring to, you may as well leave your shoes and keep on walking. It won't come off without a strong dissolvent designed to remove the toughest adhesives. There are times when we must not only rid ourselves of the glue, but we must also rid ourselves of the thing that is keeping us stuck to it.

In this book, you will discover how to speak to that situation acting as the glue and gain insight on how to dissolve that glue once and for all. It is time to *Speak To Your Glue* and gain your freedom!

Acknowledgements:

God: I thank God for all He has given me and created me to be. I thank God for life, my family, true friends, and the opportunities I have been blessed to receive.

Sylvia Madison: Mom, you are my biggest cheerleader and have always been there for me. I appreciate all you have done and sacrificed for me over the years. Because of your example, I know what it means to give from the heart, and I will continue to do so… always.

Joseph Madison: Dad, I will never forget all you sacrificed and did for me. You were there for me through so much and I thank God I could be there for you. Being your caregiver was one of the best things I have ever done. You shared the gift of writing with me which led me to so many new opportunities. I will forever appreciate you. I miss you.

Apostle Malone: I appreciate the many things you have done for me over the years, including providing the quote that changed everything for me. I share it in this book, and it will always be a part of my testimony.

Dr. Billy Jones: You have been a big part of most of the opportunities I have enjoyed, and I appreciate you. It means a lot to have you believe in me.

Sheila Gilmore: You gave me the first writing opportunity that allowed me to earn an income for my work. I will always be grateful to you for that.

Sandy Walker: You gave me the second opportunity to earn an income for my writing and I appreciate being a part of *The Gospel Truth Magazine* history. I will always be grateful to you for that.

Beverly Melasi Haag: Once again you stepped in to help me with editing and I appreciate you. I also thank you for your inspiration which helped me decide my first book series. Your support and belief in me, mean so much.

Journey Into Passion Audience: Thank you for listening. I hope I've inspired and encouraged you over that last six years, and I look forward to spending many more years together.

All Supporters: Your support means the world to me whether you tuned into the podcast, purchased a book and/or read and shared any of my writings. I truly appreciate you.

Speak to Your Glue

Before I get to the introduction, there is something especially important that we must do first. I have spoken about this frequently on my podcast, Journey Into Passion with Anika S. on Everyday Folks Radio. I am referring to the one thing we must all do before we embark on any journey, take on any life-changing goal, and do what it takes to achieve a dream. We must do our self-work.

In school, we all learned the 5 W's and the H which are, **Who**, **Why**, **What**, **When**, **Where** and **How**. As a person of faith, I added a sixth W, **Whose**. We must answer these questions for ourselves because we need a foundation to stand on as we go on these journeys. Once you have established your answers, you will gain the strength you will need when the naysayers try to deter you and fear tries to stop you.

I put the 5 W's in a certain order for a reason. Allow me to explain.

Whose – It is important for me to understand **Whose** I am, so I understand my true source. I am a child of God, and it is He who guides me. He is the one who created me, so He will be my greatest resource.

Who – God created me to be a creative woman who encourages and inspires others, while creating ideas and providing life lessons that provide assistance to those who are on journeys that lead towards ultimate destinations.

Why – My **Why** is my passion for the work. I define passion as the "can't help its." I just cannot help being an encourager. I am a creative, I love to inspire. It's my nature, and I love a good life-changing life lesson. This is the way I was created.

What – Whose, Who, and Why answer my **What**. I know why I was created, and the path God wants me to take. Understanding the gifts He gave me and the passion for them answers what I am called to do; inspire, encourage, provide life lessons, and create.

Once I discovered that, I needed to find out who I was to speak to and what I was to create. I know I love to write and have always been passionate about living my dreams. After moving forward and trying different things in these areas, the answer became clear. I am to inspire and encourage people in the areas of self-help while they move forward on their journeys towards realizing their passions; while providing life lessons that can help them achieve their goals. I have a series of books coming out soon that will help me achieve my goal of honoring all that God has provided for me, and I pray that you get what you need to do the same from this upcoming series.

Where and **When** kind of work together and there are two sides to both:

Where will you start and when will you start? The answer is the moment you have clarity and answers to whose, who, why and what. You are ready to begin.

Where will you end up and when will you get there? The answer has to do with the vision. When you see yourself in the vision you had when you reached your desired goal, and you look around to see that vision come to fruition, that's when you know the where and when have been reached.

How? – How will you start? How will you do this work? How will you gain the resources and how will you get to your ultimate destination? All the answers to the 6 W's will answer the how. You will start when you have clarity, and you will use the resources you already have based on the gifts God gave you. You will get to your ultimate destination by learning what is necessary on your path. Learn from those who are where you want to be, gather valuable information, and use strategies that make sense for your journey. I will dive more into this in the first book of my upcoming series. The book's title is *Does It Make Sense For Your Journey?*

Now let's get to it…

The Intro

"I am stuck! I cannot move forward! I am paralyzed with fear. I don't know how to get myself motivated again."

In August of 2020, my frustration with feeling stuck grew strong. I had been feeling this way for months but kept trying to move forward anyway. Then the day I dreaded came. The ideas stopped, I was no longer able to be creative, and the feeling of being paralyzed began. This was not the first time I had this wilderness experience. The last time lasted for years. I was not interested in going through that again. I had to get an answer quick. So, I prayed.

Four words dropped in my spirit that gave me the help I needed. I pray it gives you the same help.

Speak to Your Glue.

For the purposes of this book the definition for the glue is anything that you are stuck to that prevents beneficial action. To provide a visual, I am not referring to glue that you can wash off with soap and water. If you stepped into the kind of glue I am referring to, you might as well leave your shoes and keep on walking. It is not coming off without a strong dissolvent designed to remove the toughest adhesives. There are times when we must not only rid ourselves of the glue, but we also must rid ourselves of that thing that is keeping us stuck to it. More on that later.

You are not living if you are stifling who you truly are. A creative must create just like a chef must create dishes or an educator must teach. It is in your DNA, and it is how God created you. You cannot leave this earth filled with untapped talents. Your purpose for being here must be fulfilled.

In our current environment, many of us are wearing masks to protect ourselves and those around us from contracting a virus. When we get home, we remove the mask because we are no longer around others, and we can relax in our own environment. Many of us are not used to wearing the masks find it stifling and we cannot wait to take them off. It is not normal for us, and it restricts certain freedoms we have enjoyed. But to remain safe, we put them on.

There will be occasions when doing something that makes us uncomfortable is the only way to ensure we get to our ultimate realization. On our journeys, we may have to take uncomfortable steps but if it gets us to our goal, these steps are worth taking. It may also be far more comfortable to stay in your current situation even though you feel stuck, but unless you do what is necessary to become unstuck, you will never be able to realize your passions and enjoy the feeling of being fulfilled.

Moving forward, instead of using the word "dream" I am going to use the word "passion" quite often. It is one thing to dream, but there is something different about feeling passion for something. When you dream, it is in your head. When you have passion, you move forward because you simply must. Your passion is the drive.

When we stifle our passions, we are hindering a part of who we are and that becomes increasingly uncomfortable. After a while you start to get stuck in a world that is not meant for you.

That world gets increasingly difficult to get out of the longer you stay. You began with one foot stuck in the glue and eventually you became one with the glue. It overtakes you and then you end up becoming paralyzed with no way to become unstuck. At least that is what you think.

When I wrote this book, I realized I needed to be inspired first. I was stuck and had no idea how to move forward. Even though I'm always trying to inspire others, I couldn't get inspired at all for weeks. Then on a Thursday during the month of August in 2020, it became clear. God put four words into my spirit. "Speak to Your Glue." It sounded strange, but then I began to realize this was my answer to getting unstuck. My glue was causing me to be stuck in one mode all the time, and I had to let the glue know that it no longer had power over me. God had given me the power to remove myself from its grip. Once again, I felt inspired to keep moving on to the next step of my journey towards realization. This book was my next step. Stay with me and keep up with my website at www.anikamadison.net to see my future steps - including the next big one coming up very soon.

The reality is you must "Speak to Your Glue" before it overcomes you. Otherwise, it will leave you eternally stuck in a vat of it by your own creation. In the next chapter I will explain further and then present some vats that I am sure many of you will recognize.

I added the vats that we often do not discuss. We normally discuss fear, sickness, death of a loved one, demanding jobs, and other responsibilities as contributors to our being stuck.

I am introducing others. But first, the vat explanation.

Your Vat of Glue

Normally one would use a vat to hold enormous amounts of liquid because that is what the vat (tank or tub) is designed to do.

Your vat represents your way of thinking. *"Now that I've had this terrible experience, I'll never be able to move forward!"* This thinking creates an enclosed barrier that keeps you from moving forward on your journey towards realizing your passion.

Imagine yourself in a huge vat of glue you created. Because you've decided your own limitations, you reside in this vat of glue every day. At first, it just surrounds your feet. Then slowly the vat of glue grows and surrounds you. Now imagine someone coming in to pour more glue into your vat every day. The glue reaches your ankles, then your calves, and now the glue has reached your waist. Your arms and hands are free, but your feet and legs are pinned. Every day, someone comes in to pour more glue over you while they tell you all the reasons why you will never break free.

The glue poured into the vat represents the negative words you are using right now that hold you hostage. Words like stupid, fat, unattractive, slow, or busy. Yes busy. Being busy can also be the glue that keeps you stuck because you feel there is never any time to get anything done. So, you just don't even try.

Your Vat full of glue is the result of those thoughts that keeps you stuck.

Over time, you'll eventually find your way out, or you could end up creating even more vats of glue – even though your goal is to move forward. You keep creating the vats of glue every time you freeze because of fear.

Remember your past experiences when this happens. Let us discuss these vats of glue. By the end of this book, you will not only have found your way out, but discovered ways to thrive on the outside!

Vat One
The Unreasonable Timeline

The VAT AKA Your way of thinking: *"I'm so tired and busy but I must reach this goal by the end of the month. I don't know how I am going to get this done!"*

The GLUE AKA Negative Words: Busy, tired, I don't know…

Inside Your VAT FULL OF GLUE: You are stuck to the negative words which affects the way you think. Therefore, you see no way out and are unable to move forward.

Why do we constantly give ourselves these unreasonable timelines to get big things done? Why do we think it will help to reach our big goals sooner?

"I need to lose 50 pounds in two months."

"I know I am a hoarder, but I need to clean organize my two-story home this weekend."

We try to get these huge tasks done on an unreasonable timeline, and when it doesn't work, we tell ourselves we are just not capable. We end up feeling like these tasks are just impossible. The reality is, we made them impossible with unrealistic expectations.

We need to give ourselves more grace and stop buying into the idea of being able to do something well in an extremely short period of time. There is a reason we've heard, "great things take time."

Attempting to lose fifty pounds in two months means taking drastic measures that could affect your health. If you are a hoarder, you will work yourself into complete unnecessary exhaustion trying to clean and organize a two-story home in one weekend. Also, nine times out of ten, it will not get done with you trying to do it on your own.

Stop being unreasonable with your expectations. When you keep doing this to yourself, you can eventually become permanently stuck in the unrealistic vat of glue you have created for yourself.

Something to remember: Life's timeline does not negatively affect your abilities. You were born with certain talents. The way to become unstuck is to add you to your own schedule, research the normal timeline to complete the work, and be reasonable about your timeline. This takes away the added stress on your shoulders to get things done.

Vat Two
I Have Tried Too Many Times

Not only are we not allowing enough time for our passions to mature, but we are also buying into the belief that we cannot try as often as necessary.

Your VAT: *"I am mentally and physically exhausted. I am no longer interested in this because it is too hard. I don't believe this is meant for me. I just can't do this anymore!"*

Your Glue: Mentally exhausted, physically exhausted, uninterested, non-belief.

Your Glue-Filled Vat: Because you are so tired of trying and failing, your exhaustion has caused you to stop believing in yourself and your capabilities. Even though you are working towards realizing your biggest passions, you are stuck to the idea that you just do not have what it takes.

An athlete will do the same jump one hundred times and one hundred times more if that is what it takes to create a smooth landing.

It is not the amount times we try to reach a goal; it is what we learn with each try. Here is an example:

Goal: Create a five-layer specialty cake to feature in your new bakery. You are an experienced baker who has created four- and five-layer cakes before. This time you want to be known for your own special and innovative creation.

Process: Use the batter and icing you created with your special ingredients and create an astonishing design.

Result: The cake keeps toppling over and the icing tastes like any other from most bakeries.

This is your 20th attempt using the same ingredients. You question your skills and quit trying.

Your skills are not in question, the ingredients are. You can learn about other ingredients and new techniques.

Why stop trying to do something you have always wanted to do because you think you've tried too many times?

Once you have discovered your talents, your abilities should never again be in question. You are born with certain skills. They are a part of you. Stop getting stuck in this vat of glue. Get out now and discover other methods that will help you reach your goal and your passion.

Something to remember: As long as you have breath in you, you can keep trying. You will never fail if you try. You fail when you stop trying.

Vat Three
There Is Too Much Competition

It's so easy to get caught up in competition, especially on social media. You watch so many others doing what you're doing and find, in your opinion, that the majority do it better. But there is something you are not taking into consideration. None of them were born with the gifting you have, and if you give yourself enough time, you will discover they also do not have your specific ideas. The world is always looking for something new. It is looking for you.

Your VAT: *"I cannot compete. I'm not talented enough to compete with these talented people."*

Your Glue: Not competitive, not enough talent, they are more talented than I am.

Your Glue-Filled Vat: You are seeing others as the competition that will take away your passions. You believe no matter how hard you try; your work will be passed over for theirs and your hope for realization ends.

Have you heard this phrase? "What God has for you, is for you." Here's an example: You may see interior decorators whose skills are breathtaking. But if God has blessed you with these skills, look at their work as inspiration and a resource for the latest trends. Find out what your future customers are seeking and use your skills to offer them what they are looking for in a unique way. You may even start your own trend.

If God has given you a vision, He did so for a reason. That's the goal. Work towards it. I reiterate, "What God has for you, is for you."

Vat Four
Just Trying to Survive

"I am just trying to survive." You've heard those words before when someone asks another how they are doing. I was stuck doing that every day. I created this vat for myself. There were things I was doing that caused me to be stuck in situations in which I wanted to be released. I am sharing my own experiences that led me to write this book. However, I am quite sure I'm not the only one who has created this vat for themselves.

My VAT: *"I just cannot add anything else. I have too much going on and I must get to a certain goal sooner than later. My survival depends on it and nothing I have is ever good enough to get me to this goal."*

Your Glue: Never enough resources, fear of never reaching the goal, and too focused on surviving instead of thriving

Your Glue-Filled Vat: You have responsibilities, in which you've been trying to take care of for a long time. You don't want to add anything else that will prolong or destroy your efforts. You feel as though you won't survive if you do not accomplish these goals.

If you've been trying to pay off medical bills for years, the last thing you want to do is add more debt. But your current medical condition calls for you to have tests done. Unfortunately, that will cost you.

You also may want to invest in courses that will help you get closer to your business goals. Now you feel stuck. You just want to be free from debt – not add to it.

Even though taking care of your medical condition and going after your passions are both important, you create that vat of "just trying to survive." And the glue begins to pour.

Instead of creating this vat, make plans to conquer the debt. You may be missing income that can contribute to paying the debt off. You may need to change your spending habits or get help from a financial planner. You can find free resources on the internet and low-cost courses through educational platforms.

Discover how you can invest in your passions. Create a savings plan that will cover the cost of the courses. Even if it is $10 a week - That's something.

Don't be so quick to give up. Make plans.

Here are things to remember: Your health is important, and those passions will never leave you. I have been thinking about being a writer since I could form a thought as a child. It never left me, and I know it never will. So, I write! Now I am not only a published author, a blogger, a podcaster who writes my own scripts, and a freelance contributor, I also have a movie in the works. You never know just how far you can go when you give yourself a chance!

And finally, …

How Do I Speak to My Glue?

When I created the title of this book, I realized in past experiences of feeling stuck, there was a crucial step I never took. I did not speak to the situation that caused me to be stuck. I knew what it was, but I didn't deal with it.

When you step on a piece of gum, you can make the choice to just keep walking and getting stuck on the sidewalk with each step. Or you can scrape the gum off your shoe so it will no longer affect your stride.

Some of you reading this book have experienced a time when a great discovery changed your stride. That discovery helped you figure out your passions and life purpose. You were excited and leaped out of bed each morning with great anticipation. You began your stride the moment you got out of bed. There was a joy in each step. You could not wait until you were able to start working on realizing your passions.

Then life happened. A job loss or an illness. Something happened that changed the trajectory of your new journey. Your happy stride turned into delicate and fearful steps. Suddenly you no longer wanted to do anything. You got stuck and you quit.

Speak to that feeling or situation that is keeping you stuck. Speak to that thing that has left you paralyzed.

Let that situation or feeling know that you understand the following:

Who **and Whose** am I?

Then answer the following questions:

Why do I want to do this?

What am I doing?

When do I want to begin and complete the tasks it will take to realize my passion?

Where will it take me?

How will I get this done?

When I spoke to my glue, I let it know that I am a child of God who created me to inspire, encourage, and create.

Why do I want to do this?

I cannot help it. This is how God created me.

What am I doing?

I am writing, creating, inspiring, and encouraging.

When do I want to begin and complete the tasks it will take to realize my passion?

There is no need to wait. Once I made that discovery, I began my journey. I encourage you to do the same. This is when you are the most inspired. This is the best time to begin.

Where will it take me?

Wherever God wants me to go. The **Where** is the Vision God gave me. His plans for me are far better than anything I could ever dream up. My job is just to work towards that realization.

How will I get this done?

One day at a time. I will do my part, pray for direction, use the resources that make sense for my journey, and let God do the rest.

What do I say to the glue that has paralyzed me in the past?

Here is the acetone of hard-work, dedication, and most of all – belief in all that God has given me. It is time for you to dissolve and get out of my way!

I want to complete the tasks, so God sees I am ready, and the work is complete.

I am also not interested in presenting something that still needs work. If I am going to do something, it should be done in excellence. Excellence takes work and time.

On the next pages I will sum up things to remember in what I call life's important steps.

Rid Yourself of the Gripper

What is the gripper? It is that thing that has been applying the glue to your life. It could be a person, place, or thing.

If you are in a relationship with someone that is constantly standing in the way of you pursuing a dream, they are a gripper. Anytime you move forward, they produce something that causes you to take steps back or not be able to move at all. They are gripping onto you and pulling you back into your vat of glue. They want you stationary so you will not have any opportunity to leave They want to continue to receive what you provide for them. If you leave, they will lose all the things they desire the most. Therefore, each time you try to move forward, the grip gets tighter.

The gripper can also be a place. As I write this book, the world is in the second year of Covid, and many are staying home to keep themselves safe. This can be a tough thing, and if you allow it, the place you are in the most can turn into a gripper. You can feel trapped and unwilling to move forward with your plans because of fear.

You can loosen this grip by discovering new ways to safely achieve your goals. Take the time to view your dream in a different light. For example, speakers who have lost the ability to travel, speak virtually.

Physical trainers work with their clients online on Zoom, which is a great place for meetings, gatherings, and so much more. The result may not look the way you originally intended, but that is not always the true goal. It is achieving a great result and fulfilling your life's purpose. If your life's purpose is to educate, you do not always have to be in a classroom. There are online platforms looking for people to share their knowledge, so they are still realizing their life's purpose.

If the gripper is a thing, you must first identify it. Identifying the person or place is easy. You feel the glue the moment they walk in, or you step into the space. The "thing" is different. It could be an unknown gripper. Do you find yourself gravitating towards a particular thing that keeps you away from achieving a dream? Think about your typical day. Write a list of what your normally do and highlight the reoccurring items. How much time do you spend on those highlighted items? Are those items serving you and your journey towards realization or are they acting as a roadblock on your path?

Let me be clear, we need time for relaxation and enjoyment. What I am referring to are things that take away too much of your time, leaving little or no time at all for you to pursue your passions. Take time to make your list and really look at the highlighted items. Then strike a balance. Instead of spending four hours on that highlighted item, spend two on it and two hours pursuing your dream. There are many paths we take that lead us to realization of dreams. Whatever path you are on now, make sure you establish a timeline that gets you to the finish line.

Once again, there are occasions when we must not only rid ourselves of the glue, but we also must rid ourselves of that thing that is keeping us stuck to it. Do not allow the grip of a person, place, or thing to cause you to walk away from your purpose and your passions. Expand your use of the space and begin a different walk towards that purpose and passion. The realization does not always have to look exactly the way you originally pictured it; you just need to bring it from a vision into a reality.

Life's Important Steps
Remember These

Now that we've gone through examples of what your glue looks like, it is a good idea to remind ourselves of important life steps. If you have listened to my podcast, speeches or have seen any of my writings, these steps will look familiar.

I am adding them because it is important to never forget them, especially if you are speaking to your own glue and becoming unstuck.

Step One:
Discover Who You Are

For my own journey, the most important questions at the beginning are still the two most important questions I ask today as I work towards that realization.

Who am I?

And

Why do I want to do this?

My main drive is my passion which I learned from my Pastor, Apostle Carlos L. Malone, Sr., is attached to my purpose. I learned this in one of my favorite books written by him entitled, **The Road to Purpose, The Journey Beyond Potential.** In his book Apostle Malone wrote, "As a matter of fact, I believe that your purpose is strategically tied to the very gifts and talents you possess." That is my favorite quote because it changed everything for me. After reading this while in the pursuit to discovering my own life's purpose, I realized I had to look at my own gifting to realize that purpose. My gift as a writer with a creative mind who loves to encourage and inspire others, which led me to the work I am doing today.

As host of Journey Into Passion with Anika S. on Everyday Folks Radio, my goal is to inspire and encourage my listeners while providing life lessons that have helped me in my own life. The show airs the second and fourth Saturdays of the month on the Blog Talk Radio platform at www.blogtalkradio.com/everydayfolksradio.

I am grateful to my dear friend Dr. Billy Jones, Creator of the Everyday Folks Radio to be a part of the Everyday Folks Network. Soon, I will be celebrating my 100th show and my sixth year on the air.

As a writer, I love to create stories as well as create self-help guides, articles, blogs, and books like this written with the same intent as my blog talk radio show. You can see more on my websites at www.anikamadison.com and www.anikamadison.net.

My answer to the question of "Who am I" is…

I am a creative and speaker who has a passion for creating stories, encouraging, and inspiring others while providing life lessons that have benefitted my own life, and hopefully to benefit the lives of others. This is my life's purpose.

Now it is your turn.

Who are you? Think about your own gifts and talents. Then you can discover your purpose because suddenly you will realize your true passions which are attached to that purpose. You will realize it when you begin having the "I can't help its" which is my definition of passion.

My main drive has always been to pursue my passions which is why I titled my show, "Journey Into Passion with Anika S." I am literally on a journey towards realizing my passions. My goal is for my listeners to discover their own passions and find ways that will help them to realize those passions.

The year 2016 was my year of leaps. I began taking small leaps in 2015 after finally getting back to writing the year before. I took a course in screenwriting in 2014, then tried doing something new. I asked for a chance to work in marketing and began writing video scripts. Then I started writing articles. I am so grateful to Sheila Gilmore, Creator of Gilmore Marketing, and Sandy Walker, Publisher of *The Gospel Truth Magazine*, for helping me get my start and earn money as a writer.

I took even bigger leaps in 2016 when I launched my first blog at anikamadison.com. I also launched my blog talk radio show, I put my short stories on my website, and began to post personal videos. I even had my very first speaking engagement. If you had said to me in 2005 when I wrote my first book (not yet published) that years later I would be putting myself out there like this, I would have thought you were crazy. But the leaps felt amazing, and I have never looked back!

During my first speaking engagement and on my first blog, I answered the question of how to discover who you are in the form of a "To Do" list. Here is that list:

Discover the gifts God gave you.

Find out how you can use your gifts. Please note, there is no such thing as an insignificant gift!

Start your journey towards your passion today. Do your research, network, and find out what it takes to begin.

That is where I started, and it served me well. It not only taught me to take leaps, but it also led me to becoming an author of my first book, **Step By Step Caregivers Guide For Medical Appointments and Hospital Visits** now available on Amazon, which got me more speaking engagements. I've shared more of my journey on my website at anikamadison.net and anikamadison.com. Exciting ventures to come!

Pause:

Sometimes what you are reading is a lot to take in, especially if you are at the beginning of your journey into your own passions looking forward to the path to your own realization.

These are not easy journeys. There will be missteps which I like to refer to as life lessons, hardships which I like to refer to as growth spirts, and you may even have moments where you question why you ever started this journey in the first place. Let me help you on your why in Step Two.

Breathe….

Ok, pause over.

Step Two:
Discover Your Life's Purpose

Before I began my journey, I asked myself why I wanted to do this. I challenge you to do the same. Your **Who** and your **Why** will be two of the most important questions you will need answers to on this journey and here is why:

When you know who you are, no one can tell you any different. No one can come into your world and start changing things to create the person they think you should be. This information will help you work towards living the life you were meant to live. Now, there may be some things you must do to take care of your responsibilities, but do not ever give up on all the things you desire to do and are purposed to do.

Some may be wondering why the **Who** and the **Why** are more important than understanding the **What** I want. When I delved into the reasons why I wanted to become a writer and speaker, I began to get a real grasp of what I needed my journey to be, not just what I wanted from it.

I want to author a lot of books. That's great. But why? Do I have the ability to do this? I can tell people about the things I want to do but knowing who I am and why I want certain things for others as well as myself helps me stay on course.

At the beginning of my writing career, I joined a diverse group of short story writers who submitted stories for a weekly contest. At first, I received harsh comments about my work. There were members who didn't like anything I submitted.

Because I went into this group knowing I am a writer and realizing the experience of creating stories brings me joy, I did not have to struggle with what I wanted to do. I also did not struggle with quitting and buying into any notion that I was not good enough to write based on harsh comments. The writers who did not like my work became my motivators. I was after them; not to have them validate my work but to show them what I could do. I kept their comments near me while I wrote other submissions. Do you know what happened? They still didn't like what I submitted.

About four submissions later a breakthrough occurred. Two of them liked my submission! Pretty soon I had four of my worst critics liking my work and looking forward to other submissions! I turned it around because I knew I could. I knew I had it in me before I began.

When you are feeling stuck, knowing who you are and understanding your **Why** can help you every time. Before authoring this book, I had a couple of months feeling stuck. Then I got my answer! God dropped it into my spirit on Thursday, August 6th, 2020. I began writing this book that night. The words became the title of this book, ***Speak to Your Glue***. It sounded strange at first, but then it began to make sense. I had to speak to the situation that was paralyzing me. It started to become all-consuming, and I couldn't move. The blank screen became a daily occurrence which is a nightmare for a writer. Nothing was coming. I needed to speak to my glue!

Pause: Yes, I realize you may have noticed it is now a little over a year later before this book was published. Full disclosure, I had self-work to do during a difficult period. But unlike the last time I was in my wilderness experience, I did not get stuck in a vat of glue. I did my work and got back to this book. Now the book is published, and I am so excited!

You may have had or are in the middle of having the same experience. That's OK. Take care of what you must do and then work your way back. The goal is to finish. You can and if you allow your passion to take over, you will!

Pause over. Let's get to step number three.

Step Three:
Let Your Passion Drive

This step will be the shortest in this book.

You were born with a purpose, and it's your responsibility to fulfil that purpose.

My definition of passion is the "I can't help its." My passions are a part of my life's purpose. When I discovered my passions, it was clear I just couldn't help but to create, inspire, and encourage. God created me that way.

I have been encouraging and inspiring people since I was a child, and I cannot stop creating. I have been creating stories since I began to understand how to think. These things are in my DNA. All of this helped me to confirm my life's purpose.

I wrote the first draft of my first book 16 years ago, and even though I never did anything with it, the book stayed with me. The stories never left me. My passion for writing and creating has stayed with me for over 30 years.

Because this is how God created me, this feeling will never leave. In one of my blogs I wrote, "Just because you give up now, doesn't mean the dream dies. The dream will live inside of you whether you keep it going or not. The dream can either become and remain a constant nightmare, or with a lot of work, mature into an awesome reality. The choice is yours."

Do not make this step too hard. It's just that simple.

The acetone of positive words and actions has been poured onto the glue which is now dissolved. You are free to move forward.

Now It Is Time To…

Permanently Free Yourself from All Vats of Glue

There is a process to dissolving the glue, especially when it gets over your head. If you are drowning in an ocean, you must fight for your life. When you get to the surface, you must keep fighting.

That's because even though you've been able to stick your head above the water that was consuming you, doesn't mean you are out of the water. There are still more steps to take that include getting to a safer place. You cannot relax until you get to shore, so your frightening journey is not quite over.

Next you must seek medical attention to ensure your body did not incur any permanent damage. You cannot relax until all these things are complete. This will allow you to feel free enough to continue your life's journey.

Getting out of that vat of glue is step one. Doing your self-work will help you stay out. However, the remaining glue must be dissolved. Your dissolvent is creating that foundation to stand on, sealed by your self-work. Only then can you begin your journey towards realization by finding the right resources and doing the hard work.

Once you get unstuck, avoid getting stuck in the future. **Speak to Your Glue** and gain your freedom!

As always, I wish you great success on your *Journey Into Passion*.

Anika S. Madison

Let's Connect:

Linktree:

https://linktr.ee/anikaswriter

Websites:

www.anikamadison.net

www.anikamadison.com

Facebook:

www.facebook.com/journeyintopassionwithanikas

Instagram:

https://www.instagram.com/anika_s._madison/

Twitter:

https://twitter.com/AnikaVision

About the Author

Anika S. Madison is the Published Author of ***Step-by-Step Caregivers Guide For Medical Appointments and Hospital Visits*** and ***Speak To Your Glue*** both available on Amazon in Print and Kindle.

Anika is also a Transformative Speaker, Award Winning Short Story Writer, Freelance Writing Contributor, Blogger and soon to be Online Educator. She is developing a course for first time caregivers who are navigating medical appointments.

Anika S. is a member of The Bethel Church and the South Florida Writer's Association where she served on the 2018-2019 board as one of the Director at Large.

As host of Journey Into Passion with Anika S. on Everyday Folks Radio, Anika S. Madison provides her audience the same tools that have been so beneficial during her own various journeys. Her goal is to inspire, encourage, and provide information that will challenge the way her listeners normally do things so they will go from working on their passions to realizing them. You can tune into her Blog Talk Radio Show on the 2nd and 4th Saturdays of the month by going to www.blogtalkradio.com/everydayfolksradio and keep up with her upcoming work at https://www.anikamadison.net/.

Made in the USA
Columbia, SC
06 December 2024

47465018R00015